I'm GLAD I was YOUR TEACHER

written by
Brianna Frizell

Illustrated by
Diana McDermott

Text copyright © 2024 by Brianna Frizell
Illustrations copyright © 2024 by Diana McDermott.

ISBN 979-8-3255980-0-5

Library of Congress Control Number: 2024909177

12 11 10 9 8 7 6 5 4 3 2

First edition, May 2024
Published in Independence, MO USA

Text set in 'Baskerville' with hand lettering by the illustrator.
The illustrations for this book were rendered digitally.

To my sweet students. I'm so glad I was your teacher.
- BF

For my boys. I love being your teacher!
- DM

I'm glad I was teach

I'm glad that I got to see you

grow.

I'm glad that you asked questions when
there were things you didn't know.

I'm proud that you were

≶ BRAVE ≶

and always tried something new.

I'm proud that you supported each other
on days you were feeling blue.

I'm thankful for all the
lessons that we learned
throughout the year.

I'm thankful for the many
pictures and cards that now
I hold so dear.

I love you!

I'm excited for you to grow up and make your dreams come true.

I'm excited to see all the great things that I know you will do.

I'm grateful that we

LAUGHED

and shared many

SPECiaL

stories.

SOPHIA'S
FIRST DAY

I'm grateful that you could
talk to me if you ever felt any
WORRIES.

I'm happy that school
brought our classroom family
TOGETHER.

I'm happy that now our
class gets to be friends ...

I'm sad that this year
has come to a close.

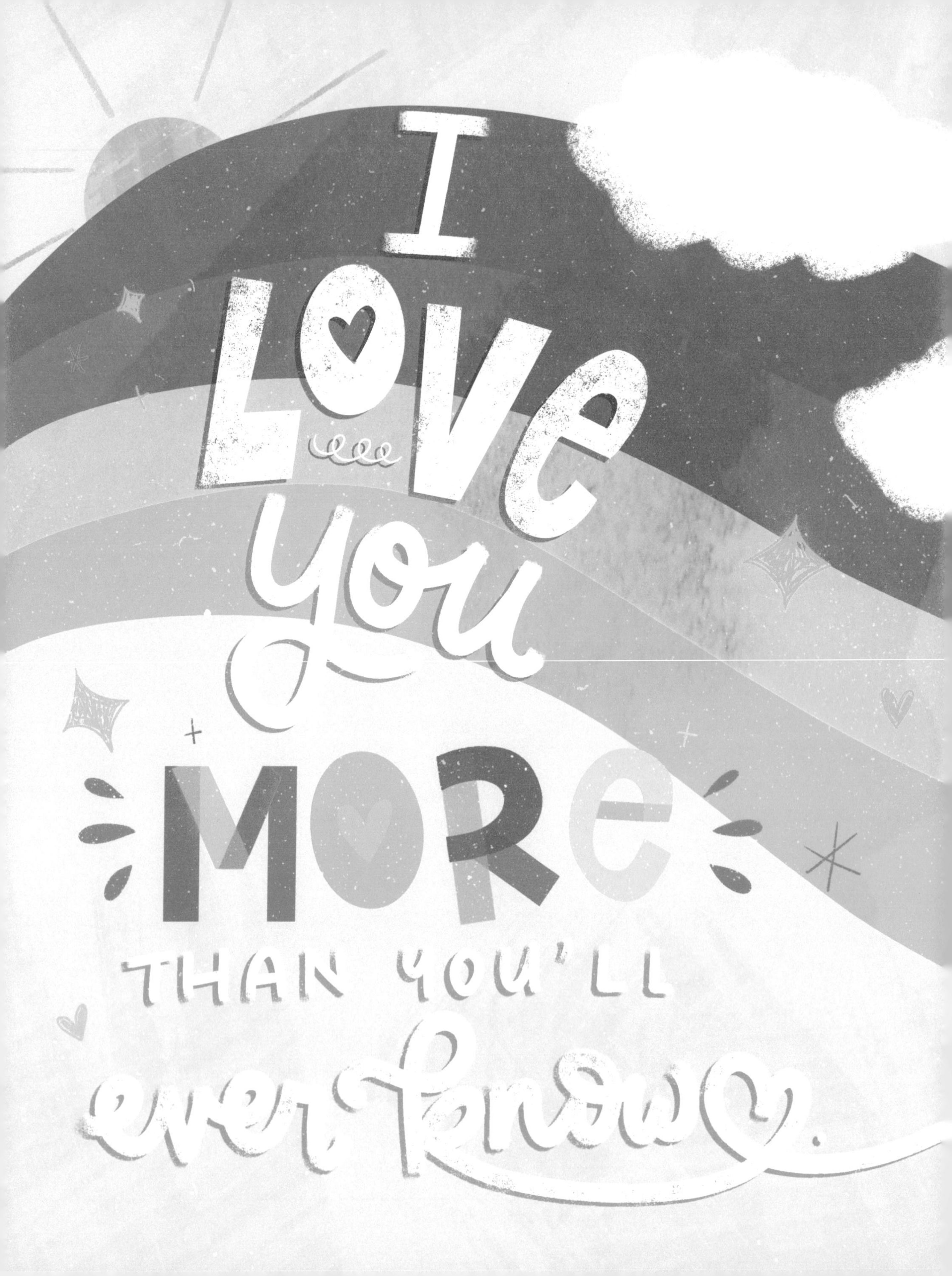
I
Love
you
MORE
THAN YOU'LL
ever know.

About the Author

Brianna is a kindergarten teacher with a love for all things colorful & fun! Growing up, Brianna dreamed of becoming an author & had so many incredible teachers who encouraged her passion for writing. In her free time you can find her creating resources for teachers, traveling to Disney World, and snuggling her fur babies.

You can keep up with her (& see cute pictures of her cats) by following along over on Instagram @teachingthetinies.

About the Illustrator

Diana's been doodling since she could hold a crayon! When she's not drawing, you may find her in the garden, jogging, or out sniffing the wildflowers in Austin, Texas where she lives with her husband and two sons. Check out more fun art stuff and kids' classes at www.dianamcdermott.com or follow along on Instagram @mymcdoodles!

Made in United States
Cleveland, OH
31 May 2025

17258190R00021